MW01503636

WHEN GOD'S GIFT COMES

Specially Wrapped

Charles R. Swindoll

INSIGHT FOR LIVING

WHEN GOD'S GIFT COMES SPECIALLY WRAPPED

By Charles R. Swindoll

Charles R. Swindoll has devoted his life to the clear, practical teaching and application of God's Word and His grace. Chuck currently is the senior pastor of Stonebriar Community Church in Frisco, Texas; but his listening audience extends far beyond this local church body. As a leading program in Christian broadcasting, *Insight for Living* airs in major Christian radio markets around the world, reaching people groups in languages they can understand. Chuck's extensive writing ministry has also served the body of Christ worldwide and his leadership as president and now chancellor of Dallas Theological Seminary has helped prepare and equip a new generation for ministry.

This booklet was taken from chapter eleven of *Parenting: From Surviving to Thriving.* Copyright © 2006 by Charles R. Swindoll, Inc., published by W Publishing Group, Nashville, Tennessee.

Published By: IFL Publishing House, A Division of Insight for Living
Post Office Box 251007, Plano, Texas 75025-1007

Editor in Chief: Cynthia Swindoll, President, Insight for Living
Executive Vice President: Wayne Stiles, Th.M., D.Min.,
    Dallas Theological Seminary
Director of Creative Ministries: Michael J. Svigel, Th.M., Ph.D. candidate,
    Dallas Theological Seminary
Editor: Mark Gaither, Th.M., Dallas Theological Seminary
Copy Editors: Jim Craft, M.A., English, Mississippi College
    Melanie Munnell, M.A., Humanities,
    The University of Texas at Dallas
Project Supervisor, Creative Ministries: Cari Harris, B.A., Journalism,
    Grand Canyon University
Project Coordinator, Communications: Dusty R. Crosby, B.S.,
    Communications, Dallas Baptist University
Proofreader: Joni Halpin, B.S., Accountancy, Miami University
Cover Designer: Kari Pratt, B.A., Commercial Art,
    Southwestern Oklahoma State University
Production Artist: Nancy Gustine, B.F.A., Advertising Art,
    University of North Texas
Cover Photo: Tari Faris

Unless otherwise identified, Scripture quotations are from the *New American Standard Bible*® (NASB). Copyright © 1960, 1962, 1963, 1968, 1971, 1972, 1973, 1975, 1977, 1995 by The Lockman Foundation. All rights reserved. Used by permission. (www.lockman.org)

Scripture quotations marked (MSG) are taken from *THE MESSAGE.* Copyright © 1993, 1994, 1995, 1996, 2000, 2001, 2002 by Eugene H. Peterson. All rights reserved. Used by permission of NavPress Publishing Group.

Scripture quotations marked (NET) are from the NET Bible®. Copyright © 1996–2006 by Biblical Studies Press, L.L.C. http://www.bible.org. All rights reserved. Scripture quoted by permission.

Scripture quotations marked (NLT) are taken from the *Holy Bible, New Living Translation.* Copyright © 1996, 2004. Used by permission of Tyndale House Publishers, Inc., Wheaton, IL 60189 USA. All rights reserved.

An effort has been made to locate sources and obtain permission where necessary for the quotations used in this booklet. In the event of any unintentional omission, a modification will gladly be incorporated in future printings.

ISBN: 978-1-57972-770-3
Printed in the United States of America

WHEN GOD'S GIFT COMES

Specially Wrapped

no evil occurs without God's sovereign permission; however, we must remember that this almighty God is also love and goodness and holiness and grace and mercy and compassion and patience and kindness. The very God who allows evil to continue on earth also subjected Himself to its terrible, destructive power along with us. The second member of the Godhead became a man in the person of Jesus Christ. And the God-man sealed the fate of evil by dying our death and rising again to offer us eternal life beyond the reach of sin and pain, sorrow and death.

While the Lord allows evil to continue, He has chosen to make the problem of pain His own. No one hates evil more than the Lord. Standing alongside the truth of God's sovereignty is His utterly holy, pure character. Holding one without the other will create an unbearable crisis of faith when we face difficulties. Now you can understand my opening sentence at the beginning of this booklet: what we believe about God determines how we live our lives. It drives everything we think and do.

Before going any further, let's be sure we're on the same page theologically. It may help for you to go back and reread those first three paragraphs.

Taking God's Sovereignty
Personally

I'd like to probe your theology with a few questions. Is God sovereign if you lose your job due to no fault of your own? Is God sovereign when you practice longer and more diligently than anyone, yet someone else wins the competition? Is He sovereign when someone less qualified than you lands the promotion for which you worked and prayed so hard? Is He sovereign when a tornado rips your house from its foundation without taking so much as a shingle from the house next door? Is He sovereign when the spouse to whom you remained faithful and put through school runs off with a colleague shortly after graduation, leaving you with the children and the bills? Is He sovereign when a drunk driver slams into your car, leaving your child a quadriplegic? How about when all of the other babies in the hospital nursery are tagged "normal," while yours has an obvious birth defect? Is He sovereign over that situation?

I don't mind admitting a time in my ministry when I could not answer yes to all of those questions. And when I could answer in the affirmative, I was slow to speak. Fortunately, the Lord has developed my theology through the trials of real life so that now I can answer enthusiastically,

"Yes! The Lord is absolutely, completely sovereign over all of those circumstances." I cannot say that I completely understand His ways, nor can I explain why He does things the way He does. Nevertheless, I acknowledge His right to rule as He pleases, and I praise Him for His character. I have finally come to the place where I can accept His sovereign rule without feeling the need to understand or explain it.

Sovereign over Questioning

Centuries ago, the Lord confronted humankind on the issue of sovereignty. The prophet Isaiah faithfully recorded His words. Please read them slowly and thoughtfully.

> "I am the LORD, and there is no
>   other;
> Besides Me there is no God.
> I will gird you, though you have
>   not known Me;
> That men may know from the
>   rising to the setting of the sun
> That there is no one besides Me.
> I am the LORD, and there is no
>   other,
> The One forming light and
>   creating darkness,

Causing well-being and creating
  calamity;
I am the LORD who does all
  these. . . .
Woe to the one who quarrels
  with his Maker—
An earthenware vessel among
  the vessels of earth!
Will the clay say to the potter,
  'What are you doing?'
Or the thing you are making say,
  'He has no hands'?"
(Isaiah 45:5–7, 9)

Most of us don't have a problem accepting the consequences of our sin or our own bad decisions. After all, we're only getting what we deserve. But when calamity strikes out of nowhere due to no failing of our own, the flesh would have us tilt our faces toward heaven and shake our fists demanding to know why. Of course, mature Christians opt for a more reasonable approach. We present our case with cool, theological reasoning, and if that doesn't work, we bargain with Him.

On one occasion several months ago, Cynthia and I were wrestling with a particular affliction and could not make sense of it. After she went to bed, I stayed up late into the night looking for

answers. I reminded the Lord of how many years I had faithfully served Him in ministry and how my conduct deserved better treatment. I paced the floor, saying, "Lord, I've faithfully served you, I've never run around on my wife, I've not stolen the church's money, I've never run off with the seminary's money (not that there's any to run away with, Lord, but we'll talk about that later), and I've always done my very best to be a good husband, father, pastor, and worshiper. How could You let this happen to me? This just isn't fair!"

Later, of course, I felt terribly stupid. And when I saw Isaiah 45:9, I shuddered a little. "Woe" is a Hebrew utterance that's not as much a word as it is a groan. It mimics the sound Jewish mourners made at funerals. "Woe to the one who quarrels with his Maker." The NET Bible renders that verse, "One who argues with his creator is in grave danger, one who is like a mere shard among the other shards on the ground!" I'm just thankful that our Maker is merciful.

He is the Potter; we are the clay. On His wheel, He does the shaping, He does the creating. He decides what clay will become a cup, or a bowl, or a pitcher. The clay doesn't shout back, "Hey! Watch it! Ouch, that hurts. No, not that. No!" With the Lord, no death is premature, though we see it that way. With the Lord,

no diagnosis comes as a surprise, although we might be shocked. And with the Lord, there are no unexpected children or unwanted pregnancies. God never looks on a child as a mistake, nor does He regard any of them as unfit, undesirable, substandard, or "defective."

We, as the clay, have no legitimate right to challenge the molding hands of the sovereign Potter.

Sovereign through Creation

Every child—every child—has been divinely formed to be a unique creation of the Father. And He makes no mistakes. King David celebrated the sovereign creation of the Lord in a song to be sung in the first person by all people.

> For You formed my inward parts;
> You wove me in my mother's
>   womb.
> I will give thanks to You, for I am
>   fearfully and wonderfully made;
> Wonderful are Your works,
> And my soul knows it very well.
> My frame was not hidden from
>   You,
> When I was made in secret,

And skillfully wrought in the
   depths of the earth;
Your eyes have seen my unformed
   substance;
And in Your book were all
   written
The days that were ordained
   for me,
When as yet there was not one
   of them.
(Psalm 139:13–16)

This God-breathed hymn of praise affirms that the Lord's creation includes no mistakes. No life is an afterthought to the Lord. Every person arrives bearing the stamp, "Made in Heaven by the Sovereign Lord," which grants each child the dignity of significance and purpose. The New Living Translation renders Psalm 139:16, "You saw me before I was born. Every day of my life was recorded in your book. Every moment was laid out before a single day had passed."

The Hebrew word alternately translated "laid out" and "ordained" is the same root word God used in Isaiah 45:9 when He said, "Woe to the one who quarrels with His *Maker*" (emphasis added). The Maker has made the moments of our lives, and each moment has a purpose. And nothing invalidates the destiny for which

we were created. Not gender, not nationality, not race, not even what we often call "birth defects."

When the Gift of Your Child Comes Specially Wrapped

How easy to accept the truth of God's sovereign design when we gaze upon a cooing newborn and see ten fingers, ten toes, two beautiful eyes and ears, and perfectly formed arms, legs, and face. But how strong is our theology when that little gift from heaven comes specially wrapped? What about when we see obvious deformity, the heartrending sight of missing or contorted limbs and distorted features? What happens to our notions of sovereign design, dignity, purpose, and destiny when we see the telltale signs of Down syndrome, spina bifida, or cleft palate? Let me push this to an extreme that nearly one out of a thousand new mothers face each year. What about the child afflicted with anencephaly, a missing or barely formed brain? How readily do we affirm that God has ordained the days—few as they are—for this little person?

My, how fragile our confidence in God's character! How quickly we discover the limits of our belief in His goodness!

I know for certain that God cherishes each life, and we can be sure that His plan includes those we would label "defective." I also know that God never wastes parents. Most new moms and dads dream of rearing the next Einstein, or Mozart, or the next Michael Jordan, and when their little one shows early signs of autism, they might be tempted to think that their child is inferior and their job is somehow less important. Profoundly autistic little boys and girls aren't likely to change the world on a grand scale (though there have been some remarkable exceptions). However, like you and me, they do impact their part of it.

Michelle Schreder, a mother of two autistic children, writes,

> What we need to learn as parents of children with special needs is how to enjoy this gift of life. It may seem impossible when we are waiting in yet another doctor's waiting room, cleaning out a feeding tube, or changing another diaper on a child well past toddler stage. But the Giver of gifts makes no mistakes. He is life; and when we appreciate the life He has entrusted to us, we come to know Him and live in His life so much better.[1]

Special-needs children do impact the world, and their parents have a much more important job than they realize. Their children challenge our most basic system of values—those beliefs that shape our understanding of human esteem, worth, and acceptance. Each encounter with a disabled or mentally challenged child becomes a crisis of principles because they remind us that the kingdom of God looks at people from a very different perspective. Michelle Schreder continues,

> We human beings constantly base a person's value and desirability on his or her looks, status, wealth, or accomplishments. . . . But clearly God does not. He welcomes everyone. . . . And He wants us, the people called by His name, to be a welcoming community as well.[2]

In one way or another and to different degrees, we are all uniquely challenged and we all need grace—the gift of complete acceptance and unqualified worth simply because God made us and values us. How important it is for us to thank God for children with special needs; without them, this comparison-obsessed world would soon have its way with our egos. And we must also thank God for the parents of these precious gifts, since these men and women are flesh-and-blood examples of the tender, unconditional, unrelenting love of God for all of us.

Biblical Answers to Difficult Questions

$\mathcal{A}$ carefully considered theology rarely ties up all the loose ends of reality. But it can provide realistic answers to tough questions. After all, theology apart from real life isn't much help. The most common questions I hear are variations of just three.

First, *did someone's sin cause my child's disability or abnormality?* The answer is complicated because it involves two very distinct issues that we frequently combine: the issues of consequences and divine punishment. Let me state this clearly: they are not the same. God is involved, but not the way we naturally think.

On the one hand, God almost always allows our actions to produce the expected consequences. Before we act, He instructs, He warns, and He frequently intervenes. He always puts us in the very best position to choose well and never allows us to be tempted beyond what we are able. Once we make our choice, however, He allows us to reap what we have sown. Using illicit drugs, abusing the use of alcohol, and smoking tobacco can damage a developing fetus, usually resulting in some kind of complication. Sins and poor choices usually produce unwanted consequences that can feel very much like punishment. However, these negative effects are not divine punishment but divine grace. Reaping the unhappy fruit of what we have sown teaches us to be responsible managers of our own freedom. God, in His grace, uses the consequences of our sins and even the sins of the world to discipline and instruct us.

On the other hand, divine punishment, though also a very real product of sin, does not come by way of natural consequences but by supernatural wrath. It doesn't come indirectly through the world but directly from God Himself. The arrival of Jesus Christ on earth began a new era—an age of grace. When Christ died on the cross, He took our sins upon Himself and endured the wrath of God on our behalf. If you have accepted His gift of grace by believing in Him, you will never experience the wrath—the divine punishment—you deserve. In grace, Jesus took it all and left *none* for you. *None*.

If, however, you choose to trust in your own goodness or hope that your good deeds will somehow purify or counteract your bad behavior — if you reject His free gift — God's wrath waits for you. When you die, or if the Lord should return before then, you will surely suffer divine punishment for your sins. But not before. Even though you continue to live in rebellion, the Lord uses the consequences of your sins and poor choices to teach you, all the while extending to you the offer of fellowship with Him.

God does not cause sin, and He does not ordain evil. But He will use the sad results of sin and poor choices for His own purposes. When Jesus and His disciples encountered a man born blind — a congenital defect — He took the opportunity to clarify this very issue.

> As [Jesus] passed by, He saw a man blind from birth. And His disciples asked Him, "Rabbi, who sinned, this man or his parents, that he would be born blind?" (John 9:1–2)

A very few Jewish sects taught that a fetus could commit sins while a great many others held that disabilities in a newborn were the result of divine retribution against the parents. It's a natural question to ask if we don't know the character of God very well. I love Jesus's answer because it bypasses the question of punishment and goes right to the heart of the issue: trust in God's sovereignty and goodness.

> Jesus answered, "It was neither that this man sinned, nor his parents; but it was so that the works of God might be displayed in him." (John 9:3)

In my experience, no one more eloquently displays the works of God than the disabled, especially when they are children. Perhaps because children with disabilities make no apology for their need and willingly accept God's intervention in their lives — much more so than proud, arrogant, able-bodied adults. I've had a number of parents say to me, "I can't number the times that I've learned something profound about God and His work as a result of having a special-needs child. I've witnessed His patience; I've experienced His love and tenderness. I've discovered the power of dependence upon Him. I've embraced simple, childlike faith. I've been forced to be patient . . . to slow my pace and walk a little more carefully because of the time it takes to accommodate our child's needs. I have experienced life in ways I never would have otherwise."

Joni Eareckson Tada, a marvelous example to all of us, writes with clear-thinking honesty,

God doesn't just watch [harm] happen—he lets it happen. What is accidental from our perspective was specifically allowed by God. He who holds all things together must sustain the very molecules of the brick and axehead as they fly toward their mark (Colossians 3:17). . . .

Evil can only raise its head where God deliberately backs away—always for reasons that are specific, wise, and good, but often hidden during this present life. . . .

God sees the evil already there and steers it to serve his good purposes and not merely Satan's viperous ones. It's as if he says, "So you want to sin? Go ahead—but I'll make sure you sin in a way that ultimately furthers my ends even while you're shaking your fist in my face." This is why we can accept troubles as ultimately from God even when the most dreadful people deliver them.[3]

As soon as Jesus finished correcting the theology of His disciples, He declared, "I am the Light of the world" (John 9:5), and then He gave the blind man sight. In this one act, Jesus demonstrated His authority over disabilities, sin, bad theology, the temple, the Sabbath, even the self-absorbed Pharisees who opposed Him. He had this opportunity because a little baby came into the world without the ability to see. God did not cause the baby's affliction; He gave it divine purpose before anything had been created.

A second question I often encounter: *How is God involved in birth defects and disabilities?*

We have established that the Lord is absolutely sovereign, yet He does not directly cause bad things to occur, such as physical and mental disabilities. However, they do occur by His permission, and He does directly ordain their purpose within His plan.

In Exodus 3–4, Moses stood before the burning bush arguing with God. He had spent his first forty years honing his natural abilities in Egypt, expecting to become the savior of Israel, perhaps by leading a military revolt against the Pharaoh. He saw an Egyptian abusing a Hebrew and took it upon himself to liberate his brother by murdering the attacker. He acted on his own initiative, in his own strength, expecting gratitude in return. Instead, the Lord remained silent, the Hebrew scoffed, and the Egyptian authorities sought his life.

Moses spent the next forty years of his life exiled, content to use his natural leadership skills on his father-in-law's flocks, resigning himself to the fact that he blew his big chance to rescue Israel. Then, at 80 years of age, he heard the Lord call to him. Standing barefoot before the eerie glow of God's presence, he heard the command, "Come now, and I will send you to Pharaoh, so that you may bring My people, the sons of Israel, out of Egypt" (Exodus 3:10). And so the argument began, during which we learn that Moses had a disability.

Moses first offered a number of reasons that God's plan wouldn't work, which the Lord countered by promising him miraculous abilities. After Moses exhausted all other excuses, he fell back to his last line of defense. "Master, please, I don't talk well. I've never been good with words, neither before nor after you spoke to me. I stutter and stammer" (Exodus 4:10 MSG). His actual words might have been, "I-I-I am s-s-s-s-s-slow of m-mouth aaaaand s-s-low of t-t-t-tongue." We forget that fact when we think of Moses, the leader of the Exodus. The man had a speech impediment, which he used as an excuse to keep from obeying God.

The Lord's response? Read it very carefully.

> "Who has made man's mouth? Or who makes him mute or deaf, or seeing or blind? Is it not I, the LORD? Now then go, and I, even I, will be with your mouth, and teach you what you are to say." (Exodus 4:11–12)

In other words, "Moses, you're talking to the Lord of mouths. Your disability is no surprise to Me, and it won't thwart My plans. In fact, your stammering tongue is part of My divine, sovereign strategy—always has been."

If your child was born blind, he or she was formed that way under the supervision of the Lord for His purposes and for His glory. It's not your fault; it's God's sovereign plan. Keeping this perspective can make all the difference for you and your child.

When I was a student at Dallas Theological Seminary, I got to know a very gifted young man a year or two behind me in his training. I remember thinking that his ability in the pulpit would give him a bright future in ministry. I have since lost touch with him, but we enjoyed a nice friendship. I also remember that he had a birthmark that ran from his hairline, across his nose, down his cheek, jaw, and neck. It looked as though someone had dipped two fingers in bright red paint and smeared it down his face. He intrigued me because he seemed to have no self-consciousness. His bold, confident presence revealed a security and even a sense of humor that few possess. One day I decided to come right out and ask him about it.

He smiled and said, "Actually, I have my dad to thank. For as long as I can remember, he used to say, 'Son, just before you were born that's where the angel kissed you. None of the other kids have that mark, and so that's how I know you're mine.'" He said, "You know, Chuck, it got to where I felt a little sorry for people who didn't have a red mark across their faces."

A third question I often hear: *If God is sovereign and hates evil, why would He allow this to happen to me, to us, to my family? Why does God wait to put an end to evil? Why does He not do it now?*

I find Paul's doxology in Romans 11 to be helpful. He raises his hands in praise and writes with much passion:

> Oh, the depth of the riches both of
> the wisdom and knowledge of God!
> How unsearchable are His judgments

and unfathomable His ways! For who has known the mind of the Lord, or who became His counselor? Or who has first given to Him that it might be paid back to him again? For from Him and through Him and to Him are all things. To Him be the glory forever. Amen. (Romans 11:33–36)

The answer to the third question is: *no one knows.* No one knows why God chooses as He does and acts as He does. Why one family's life would be marked by tragedy and another remains seemingly free of tragedy. Why disease and illness would nearly destroy one family while another stays healthy and strong. Or why the Lord doesn't come now to conquer the world and destroy evil and remove disabilities forever.

If I were able to answer these three questions with complete satisfaction, we would have other questions to take their place. At some point, even the most brilliant and accomplished theological minds must cast aside their books and notes to praise the Lord. And they choose to praise Him for His character in the absence of tidy resolutions. To this last question and a hundred more like it, I openly admit, "I don't know." But where my knowledge fails, I can trust the Lord's sovereignty and goodness, ultimately, to make everything right.

Perspectives

$\mathcal{I}$ began this booklet with the bold claim that our theology affects everything about us—our decisions, how we will react to the circumstances of life, even how we will behave toward one another. Right thinking demands right action.

To Those Who Have Special-Needs Children

$\mathcal{I}$ want to be very, very careful as I write this because I am not a parent of a disabled child, though I am a grandfather of one. My wife and I continue to watch our daughter endure the sadness, heartache, frustration, and sheer exhaustion of rearing an autistic son. So my experience as a grandparent qualifies me to sympathize with better-than-average knowledge, but I cannot offer firsthand advice.

To you, I hope you will trust God each day for new strength. I hope you will not hesitate to admit your weakness, to allow yourself frustration and sadness, and to request the help of others often. In many ways, the job requires superhuman energy, superhuman patience, and superhuman diligence and wisdom. And because you generally get the job done fairly well, you can easily forget that you're only human.

To Those Who Do Not Have Special-Needs Children

$\mathcal{L}$et's reach out, even if we don't know how or don't know what to say.

I notice that people who encounter those who are disabled tend either to stare uncompassionately from a distance or to ignore them completely. Very few people talk to disabled people or the people helping them or even their parents. And I understand why. We're afraid of offending or saying something that will embarrass either ourselves or the other person. For example, in a church where I formerly served, I happened to be standing nearby when a woman pushing her husband in a wheelchair approached an usher for a worship folder. The usher held out a folder and said, "Good morning. This is for you. Does he want one?"

She very politely replied, "Why don't you ask him?"

Of course, the embarrassed usher—a fine, sensitive gentleman—was mortified over his thoughtless question. After he confirmed that the husband wanted one and saw the couple to their seat, he wanted to crawl into a hole somewhere on the dark side of the moon.

No one wants to offend or feel embarrassed, but the encounter was better than the alternative. He risked and blundered . . . and learned. For all its awkwardness, it involved an authentic human interaction that disabled people often crave. For sure, next time that usher will know to look in those eyes and address a person in a wheelchair directly.

Let me encourage you to reach out. Engage. Risk saying or doing the wrong thing. Begin by treating a disabled person as you would any other person, then as you observe or as he or she directs, adjust to accommodate the disability. If you goof, apologize and accept his or her grace. Judging by the conversations I've had, they much prefer your well-intentioned efforts to being ignored.

May I be bold here? *We are all disabled.* Some disabilities are more difficult to hide than others, and most of us do a great job keeping our disabilities safely concealed (which is a major problem!). But we all have special needs.

Thankfully, we have a Savior who looks directly at each one of us, seeing us as we are and valuing us as His own prized creation.

We Are Here for You

Parenting a child with special needs is exhausting and lonely. The grief over your child's struggles, the sense of loss you feel for what might have been, and the personal heartaches that permeate your daily life can be overwhelming. But you are not alone.

Insight for Living's Special Needs ministry has been carefully designed to provide you with listening ears, sources of comfort, and many resources to guide you along your journey with the "specially wrapped gift" God has entrusted to you.

Please don't hesitate to contact us. We would love to get to know you and your child, standing with you, praying for you, and helping you in any way we can. Give us a call at (972) 473-5016, e-mail us at specialneedsministry@insight.org, or write to us at the following address:

Insight for Living
Special Needs Ministry
Post Office Box 269000
Plano, Texas 75026-9000

If you desire to find out more about knowing God and His plan for your life, contact us. Insight for Living provides staff pastors and women's counselors who are available for free, written correspondence or phone consultation. These seminary-trained men and women have years of pastoral experience and are well-qualified guides for your spiritual journey.

Please feel welcome to contact our Pastoral Ministries department by using the information below:

Insight for Living
Pastoral Ministries Department
Post Office Box 269000
Plano, TX 75026-9000
(972) 473-5097, Monday through Friday
8:00 a.m.–5:00 p.m. Central time
www.insight.org/contactapastor

Endnotes

1. Michelle Schreder, *The Unexpected Gift* (Sisters, Ore.: VMI, 2004), 8. Used by permission.

2. Schreder, *The Unexpected Gift*, 118.

3. Joni Eareckson Tada and Steven Estes, *When God Weeps: Why Our Sufferings Matter to the Almighty* (Grand Rapids: Zondervan, 1997), 83, 85–86. Copyright © 1997 by Joni Eareckson Tada and Steven Estes. Used by permission of Zondervan.

Ordering Information

When God's Gift Comes Specially Wrapped

If you would like to order additional booklets or request other products, please contact the office that serves you.

United States

Insight for Living
Post Office Box 269000
Plano, Texas 75026-9000
USA
1-800-772-8888
Monday through Thursday,
7:00 a.m. – 9:00 p.m. and
Friday, 7:00 a.m. – 7:00 p.m. Central time
www.insight.org

Australia, New Zealand, and South Pacific

Insight for Living Australia
Post Office Box 1011
Bayswater, VIC 3153
AUSTRALIA
1 300 467 444
www.insight.asn.au

Canada

Insight for Living Canada
Post Office Box 2510
Vancouver, BC V6B 3W7
CANADA
1-800-663-7639
www.insightforliving.ca

United Kingdom and Europe

Insight for Living United Kingdom
Post Office Box 348
Leatherhead
KT22 2DS
UNITED KINGDOM
0800 915 9364
www.insightforliving.org.uk

Other International Locations

International constituents may contact the U.S.
office through our Web site (www.insight.org),
mail queries, or by calling +1-972-473-5136.